Sebastian Gets the Hiccups

Written by Jenny Feely
Illustrated by Alex Stitt

"Oh no!" said Sebastian.
"I've got the hiccups ...
I've got the hiccups, Mom.
What should I do?"

"Hold your breath and count
to one hundred," said Mom.

So Sebastian tried holding his breath
and counting to one hundred.

"I tried holding my breath
and counting to one hundred,
but I've still got the hiccups."

"Drink from the wrong side
of a glass," said Dad.

So Sebastian tried drinking
from the wrong side
of a glass.

5

"I've got the hiccups, Grandma,"
said Sebastian.
"I tried holding my breath
and counting to one hundred.
I tried drinking water from
the wrong side of a glass.
But I've still got the hiccups."

"Try blowing into a paper bag,"
said Grandma.

So Sebastian tried blowing
into a paper bag.

Hic!

8

"I've still got the hiccups, Mom,"
said Sebastian. "What can I do?
I've already tried lots of things."

"I held my breath and counted
to one hundred.
I drank from the wrong side of a glass.
I blew into a paper bag."

"Try rubbing your tummy and patting
your head at the same time," said Mom.

So Sebastian tried.
He patted
and rubbed
and patted
and rubbed.

Pat here.

Rub here.

Sebastian saw Grandpa.
"You've got the hiccups,"
said Grandpa.

"Try standing on your head.
It always works for me."

So Sebastian tried standing on his head.

"What are you doing, Sebastian?"
asked Isabella.

"I'm standing on my head,"
said Sebastian. "I've got the hiccups.
I've tried everything.
I held my breath
and counted to one hundred.
I drank water from the wrong side
of a glass.
I blew into a paper bag.
I even rubbed my tummy
and patted my head.
I'm going to have the hiccups
forever!"

12

"BOO!" yelled Isabella.

15

"What did you do that for?"
Sebastian asked angrily.

"You'll see," said Isabella.

Sebastian waited.

"I don't have the hiccups anymore,"
said Sebastian. "It worked!"

"But now I have them!" groaned Isabella.